ELLE DECOR
PORTFOLIOS

LIVING ROOMS

Cover: photo © Marianne Haas
Reportage Marie-Claire Blanckaert

Copyright © 2003 Filipacchi Publishing for the present edition
Copyright © 2001 Editions Filipacchi, Société SONODIP – *Elle Décoration*, for the French edition

Translated from French by Simon Pleasance and Fronza Woods
Copyedited by Matthew J.X. Malady

ISBN: 2 85018 646 5

Color separation: Hafiba

Printed and bound in France by Clerc

LIVING ROOMS

filipacchi
publishing

The living room is perhaps the one room that is most central to the "home." Because it is the room we live in and the place where we entertain those we invite into our home, today's living room must be both convivial and comfortable. We have come a long way from the pomp and ceremony of the reception room of the early 20th century, where guests would conduct themselves as salon etiquette dictated, perched on uncomfortable chairs.

Indeed, in the modern era, living rooms have become known as places that are good to live in, and where everyone likes to linger. They offer a chance to express refinement and to show off different decorative styles, using every possible opportunity to come up with myriad combinations that can be created by combining sofas and settees, armchairs and coffee tables, organized around a bookcase or arranged beside a fireplace.

Some designers dare to introduce eccentricity into these living spaces, happily mixing different styles and hues. Others stress simplicity and softness by creating sumptuous white living rooms.

This book invites you to venture not only among the great names in interior design and fashion, but also into the homes of ordinary people who have cleverly arranged their living rooms with both taste and imagination. The hope is that within these pages you will find your own sources of inspiration.

CONTENTS

SOFA NOOKS

THESE ARE PLACES CONDUCIVE TO CHATTING AND RELAXING WITH
FRIENDS. CORNER SETTEES, BANQUETTE SEATS, CLUB CHAIRS AND
CHAISE LOUNGES, EMBELLISHED WITH CUSHIONS AND PLAIDS. SOFA
NOOKS OPT FOR COMFORT AND WARMTH IN A MOST ELEGANT WAY.

Above. Anthony Collett chose a bold, neo-Baroque style to enliven the living room of an old London house. A burst of powerful colors gives this room its vibrant, cheerful feel. The walls are covered with gold leaf, and the two wing chairs are upholstered in military baize, with shawls and cushions designed by G. Flower. The curtains are in red and purple velvet, while the under curtains are in bright yellow cotton. **Left.** The bold-striped sofa was designed by Collett himself. The cushions are by Julia Pinès. To the right of the sofa, an early 20th-century ecclesiastical table.

Above. In his Paris home, young antiques dealer Alexandre Biaggi shows his flare for combining objects in a most unexpected way. In the living room, the atmosphere harkens back to the 1950s and '60s. Two Serge Mouille lights have been hung from the ceiling. The matching, zebra-striped cushions and two candlesticks complete this play of symmetry. Set no less shrewdly on the coffee table are ashtrays from the Capron studio, which call to mind the ceramics of Vallauris.

Right. East meets West, in style, here at this Istanbul residence where Anouska Hempel has juggled with harmonies in ginger, black and stone. This area of the living room also doubles as a screening room. The screen is cleverly concealed beneath the ceiling, above the windows. The sofas in thick, dark-colored Indian cotton, are partly covered with cashmere rugs. On the low chest tables, a black lacquer tray, circa 1930, plays host to two silver salvers holding Moroccan matchboxes.

SOFA NOOKS

Interior decorator Julie Prisca
has set the living room of
her Normandy home in sunny
colors. The furniture, which
she designed, fits perfectly
with the saffron-yellow walls
and the beams painted a
delicate, lagoon green. The sofa
is covered in bright, red cloth.
And on the covered armchairs,
a wool and angora buttoned
plaid. The top of the coffee
table is in oak that was gouged
out to create this handsome
motif. At the back of the room
stands an impressive piece of
regional furniture made of
fruitwood. Seagrass carpeting
covers the floor and provides
the perfect finishing touch to a
room that evokes the colors and
textures of a sunny marshland.

Above. Decorators David Champion and Anthony Collett have reorganized the space of this large London apartment, and designed much of the furniture in it, to boot. The 17th-century fireplace is set off by a very 20th-century photo of Pablo Picasso, which was taken by Irving Penn. Picasso's fixed gaze cuts through the creamy white hues of the living room. On either side of the fireplace, there are Collett-and Champion-designed loudspeakers doubling as stands for ancient Greek vases. The yellow- and grey-striped silk fabric of the chaise lounge—designed by Christopher Gibbs—picks up the stripes of the curtains. The sofa, tables and lamps were also designed by Collett and Champion.

Right. In a village house on the Ile de Ré, on France's Atlantic coast, an L-shaped sofa surrounds a coffee table formed by two Bertoia benches set side by side. The lamps are by David Hicks. On the windows, venetian blinds with thin wooden slats filter the light. At the far end of the living room, there is an elegant spiral staircase imported from London.

SOFA NOOKS

By giving free rein to the color white—combined with his trademark black stripes—interior designer Frédéric Méchiche has created new, strong lines as the main theme for the living room in this Paris duplex. The floor is oak parquet. On the wrought iron coffee table, we see a pair of candlesticks by Méchiche and a sculpted bowl by Eric Schmidt. To the left, on the column at the foot of the stairs, Méchiche has hung a painting by Jean-Claude Agostini. The bronze on the mantelpiece is by Barye. Next to it is a Survage drawing.

Left. Henri Becq, designer and founder of the Modénature furniture store in Paris, lives in an apartment featuring a condensed version of the style that has earned him such success—a simple, sober place that is easy to live in. In the living room, two chaise lounges in string linen act as sofas. Cotton cloth curtains by Chantal Benoist were chosen to dress up the windows. They can be drawn from wall to wall along the fixed traverse rod. The standard lamps were designed by Karl Kroener for Modénature. On the wall, collages by Ariane Lassaigne.

Above. Monic Fisher, founder of the Blanc d'Ivoire company, has chosen a timeless, easy-to-live-in style for her Saint-Germain-des-Prés home. The two large sofas in the main living room are covered in linen. On the Le Corbusier leather sofa, a sand-colored quilt by Blanc d'Ivoire. On the coffee table by Gae Aulenti, bronze Japanese vases and silver-plated bowls make up the tablescape. Against the far wall, between the two French windows, there is a Kamakura sculpture by Georges Jeanclos.

19

Above. The generous living room Philippe Starck created for his house near Paris maintains the feeling of a loft. Much of the room is taken up by a huge sofa of French-polished cherry wood, designed by Jean-Denis Coat. Plump cushions with white linen covers are piled deep along the sofa. Over the windows, a striking frieze made of colored windowpanes. Just above that, a shelf that runs around three sides of the room.

Right. Interior decorator Agnès Comar has added just what is needed in terms of comfort and refinement to this small living room-*cum*-library. A pair of sofas in cashmere and suede stand on a wool hemmed linen carpet. Black cushions discreetly echo the color of the lampshades. On the shelf, we find one or two old pictures by Le Valais and some photos. The silver-plated lights are by Agnès Comar.

Above. This private, 19th-century mansion was decorated by Hubert Le Gall. The living room was divided so as to create two independent areas made one by the style. Above the sofa, a work by Tamara de Lempicka is flanked by bronze cogwheels by Le Gall. In the foreground, the main part of the living room has been furnished with 1940s-style armchairs and lamps.

Right. The owner of this apartment in Lyons entrusted architect Rémi Tessier with the task of decorating. The leather and woven linen sofa was made by Tessier. Above it, two pictures are set on a small shelf designed specifically for them. To the right, on the stone table, a lamp made of wenge wood with a silk shade.

SOFA NOOKS

A distinctive feature of
this living room, designed
by Agnès Comar, is a splendid
fireplace made of large stones
in the purest Adirondack style.
On either side of it are
sofas covered with terry.
The four mahogany lamps
behind the sofas are by Nobilis.
The curtains are made of white
baize, on which Comar has
applied slanting stripes.
Beneath the mezzanine,
a traditional piece of painted
furniture by Le Valais.

AROUND
COFFEE TABLES

AT THE CENTER OF THE LIVING ROOM, FOR ALL TO LOOK AT, THE
COFFEE TABLE IS OFTEN USED FOR DISPLAYING FLOWERS, BOOKS AND
MUCH LOVED OBJECTS. THERE IS NO LACK OF IMAGINATION WHEN IT
COMES TO MAKING USE OF MATERIALS. INTERIOR DECORATORS HAVE
A FIELD DAY WITH: BAMBOO, BRONZE, GLASS, OAK AND SYCAMORE.

Left. In Manuel Canovas'
living room, a rather whimsical
coffee table made of bronze
and glass, sculpted by
Diego Giacometti.
The subtle, yet bright colors
of the moquette show off this
table to great advantage.

Above. A metal bed from
India serves as a coffee table
in Agnès Comar's home in
Provence. On either side of
the sofa, tables covered with
long tablecloths are adorned
with matching wooden lights,
which Comar designed.

AROUND
COFFEE TABLES

This huge coffee table, with
its sober elegance, is made
of ash wood tinted black.
Because of its color and its
design, it goes well with many
different styles of decoration.
Amongst other objects on
display, to the right of the table
is a César thumb by Daum.
The Louis XVI mahogany
armchair is by Moreau.
Above the sofa, a copy of
a painting by José Conrado
Roza, of the late 17th-century
Portuguese school.

Left. This table, designed by Olivier Gagnère for Artelano, is distinctive for its simplicity. The bleached oak blends with the colors of the 1930s carpet and those of the screen. Both were flea market finds.

Above. In this collector's living room, a decorative style made up of a thousand and one precious objects. In the middle, the coffee table by Jacques-Emile Ruhlmann consists of two tabletops, one above the other.

The armchairs around it are by the same designer. The display cabinet is by Prinz, and the table lamp and floor lamp are by Tiffany. The glassware collection is by Daum, and the glasses are from Venice.

AROUND
COFFEE TABLES

A mixture of styles and an
intermingling of periods is
evident in Axel Vervoordt's
castle near Antwerp. On the
flattened bamboo coffee table,
designed by the antiques
dealer-*cum*-interior designer,
there are symbolic ivory objects
from the Ming period,
a rectangular ceramic tray
from the Han period,
and a precious brown-glaze
vase with a bird's head spout
dating to the Khmer period.
The armchair from the
Louis XIII period is covered
with antique wool fabric.
On the table and in the
18th-century pine cupboard
from the Rhineland, a
collection of Sukhothai pottery.

Left. In the Provençal home of a collector, we find this generously proportioned Anglo-Indian coffee table. Much of it is covered with fine books, which seems in keeping with the numerous works of art lining the walls. The 18th-century Provençal armchairs, together with the sofa, the carpet and the lampshades, all in warm colors, form a harmonious whole.

Above, right. For these coffee tables, Yves Taralon has used two old X-shaped stands, on which he has laid birchwood tops. The 17th-century stone fireplace is flanked by vases from Anduze.

Below, right. On the oak parquet floor, a practical table made for friendly gatherings. The walls are painted yellow and ochre, and the sofa is lit by two wrought iron floor lamps.

AROUND
COFFEE TABLES

In the living room of this early 20th-century castle in Flanders, the oak floor made of freight train planks. On it, Lionel Jadot has arranged a Louis XVI daybed and a carpet made from a Berber tent. This young interior designer has chosen subtle shades of color—such as pale gray and beige—which highlight the eclectic collection of objects and furniture. Jadot designed all the seating, which was subsequently made in the Vanhamme family business.

Here, the coffee table and trestle table behind the sofa rest on a studio parquet floor made of broad, dark planks. The tables were designed by Laurent Bourgois. On the far side of the room is a Christian Liaigre armchair with footrest. The various lamps are by Yves Halard, Christian Liaigre and Nobilis. The fireplace was made by Gazzola and is based on a Laurent Bourgois design.

AROUND COFFEE TABLES

Above. In this living room, nestled beneath a mezzanine, interior designer Rémi Tessier has created a play of right angles and straight lines. The table is made of dark sycamore and was designed by Patricia and Philippe Hurel. It stands out because of its elegant simplicity, and sits gracefully on a plum-colored rug. Philippe Hurel also designed the chaise lounge, as well as the oak table. The chairs are covered in a tawny leather, and the low, armless easy chair is covered in tobacco-colored wild silk. In the back, to the right, an oil painting by Pincemin. The lamp to the left was created by Tessier for Jean-Michel Delisle.

Above. In Ixelles—the comfortable, residential area of Brussels—we find a living room full of light and sharp contrasts. The design of the room relies on faultless finishing touches orchestrated by interior designer Axel Verhoustraeten to achieve a decidedly contemporary effect. The wooden coffee table is a Christian Liaigre creation, as is the jute fabric covering the sofa. The floor lamp was designed by Verhoustraeten. On the wall, a series of desert photos by Sylvie Durimier. Easy living is the prevailing theme in this living room that places great emphasis on wood and white.

AROUND
COFFEE TABLES

In this living room, featuring
superb 17th-century oak
woodwork, a coffee table with
a Poillerat travertine top is
supported by globes. It stands
on a carpet created by Arbus.
To the left, the oak stools and
bronze and leather armchair
are also Arbus creations.
Behind the sofa, Poillerat
wall lights illuminate a picture
of a Japanese notable.
The matching armchairs are by
Arbus, and the furniture comes
from the Yves Gastou gallery.

Above. This contemporary living room displays an oblong coffee table with rounded lines, which contrast with the right angles of the furniture. The wood and metal staircase, designed by Julie Prisca, leads to the attic. Near the French windows, we see a leather armchair with white fabric cushion covers. The desk, to the rear, is made of wood and metal, and in front of it stands a delicate banquette made of metal with white cloth cushion coverings. Facing the fireplace—which is framed by a broad, gray metal surround—are metal and white fabric armchairs, a sofa and upholstered chairs. All of this furniture was designed by Julie Prisca. Soft, subtle colors

create a charming and peaceful atmosphere.

Above. The interior design of this Parisian living room is based on a play of contrasts between the light walls and the dark materials used for the curtains and sofas.

The decoration is also informed by the horizontal lines of the furnishings and fittings—in particular the mirror, which echoes the lines of the Catherine Memmi coffee table. The mirror, the pouffe and the chrome-plated floor lamp are also by Memmi. The Christian Liaigre sofa is covered with a woolen fabric designed by Bisson Bruneel. The small bunches of flowers arranged on the table add a delicate splash of color.

AROUND
COFFEE TABLES

In this sun drenched living room
of a Paris apartment. a subtle
balance is achieved between
ivory. red and black hues.
The sofa is flanked
by a bench made by Nelson
and an occasional table by
Jean Royère. Near the fireplace
is a work by Jean Arp entitled
"Sculpture de Silence." On the
walls. the bright red of a Lucio
Fontana canvas and a pleated
Piero Manzoni anachrome.

Above. Yves Gastou and Jean Galvani are responsible for the look of this large Toulouse apartment. Gastou brought together a collection of neoclassical pieces from the 1940s, and Galvani introduced a touch of spare design to the premises. The living room is dominated by the impressive Arbus bookcase made in the 1950s. The marble coffee table was designed by Gae Aulenti. The furniture is made of oak. A pair of Venetian glass lamps from the 1940s stand on the tables beside the sofa.

Above. A play of symmetries prevails in this living room in a triplex converted by architect Rémi Tessier. The central axis is formed by the two bamboo coffee tables. The furniture is decked out in both muted and dazzling colors, which contrast with the beige hue of the walls painted in marble powder. The sofas, in leather and woven linen, and offset by embroidered cushions, were designed by Tessier, as was the red bench. On either side of the window with its linen curtains, a pair of black oak bookshelves that were also designed by Tessier.

49

AROUND THE
FIREPLACE

ALL IT TAKES IS THE MAGIC OF A WOOD FIRE, AND SUDDENLY A CITY
APARTMENT CAN BE TRANSFORMED INTO A COUNTRY HOME. WHETHER
THEY ARE MADE OF MAHOGANY OR MARBLE, STONE OR PINE, FIREPLACES
ADD A FRIENDLY, WELCOMING TOUCH TO LIVING ROOM DECORATION.

Left. Above this 19th-century marble fireplace, against a stone background painted in trompe-l'œil by Alain Ozanne, Jacques Leguennec has arranged various objects: a 17th-century wooden mannequin, a chimaera, marble and alabaster ruins, and Pascale Laurent watercolors.

Above. This stone fireplace, designed by Guy Bontemps in the 1930s style, is framed from floor to ceiling by two long light strips in black ironwork. The color scheme for the living room was inspired by the 1930s vases created by David.

Above. In the home of architects Jean-Louis and Mado Mellerio, this very distinctive shade and uneven effect for the fireplace was achieved by mixing concrete with clay. On either side of the fireplace stand a sofa and an armchair designed by Jean-Louis and Mado. Both are covered with a brightly colored fabric by Zoltan. The Ettore Sottsass sculpture comes from the Yves Gastou gallery.

Right. In front of Kenzo's Japanese bedroom, the fireplace is encircled by a metal, mesh fire guard. It stands center stage, asserting itself as the main feature of the decor. To the left, a traditional Japanese lantern.

AROUND THE FIREPLACE

Left. Joëlle Mortier Vallat
wanted to transform her
extremely classical, white
marble, 19th-century fireplace,
so she painted it in leopard spot
trompe-l'œil. A jumble
of wonderful things are on
display here—including an
architect's light from 1910,
a bullfighting lithograph by
Picasso, a pair of American arts
and crafts-style candlesticks,
and a 19th-century bronze
Japanese vase.

Right. An ingenious idea
to revamp and rejuvenate
a classical fireplace:
Paint it white. Here, a
perfect opportunity to
display a collection of
Staffordshire pottery.

Left. The home of couturier Joseph features the elegance and simplicity of a marble fireplace. A triple recess merges it with the wall—a modern and original design.

Above. In the home of interior designer Daniel Kiener, the fireplace set into the wall seems to be a natural extension of the bookshelves. In the foreground, English armchairs from India.

AROUND THE FIREPLACE

Left. Maïmé Arnodin's fireplace,
made up of mirror shards,
was designed by César.
The sculpture, entitled "La
Poulette," is also a César work.
The small chain curtains
acting as a fire guard were
commissioned from San Diego.

Right. In the home of
Patrick and Yveline Frèche,
the raised fireplace is made of
painted brick. A broad surround
offers plenty of room on either
side of the hearth for sculptures
and photos. The coffee table
is made of painted ash.

Above. An amusing idea for
this Baroque-inspired fireplace
in the home of the artist
Charles Matton: In the guise
of a fire guard, a picture
shields the hearth.
Right. This fireplace is
flanked by two mahogany
bookcases with ebony inlay.

They were designed by
Anouska Hempel, who has
hung 19th-century prints
above the mantle that depict
Greek philosophers. The
cashmere rugs and cushions
bring out the warm atmosphere
created by the harmony
of ginger and black.

AROUND THE FIREPLACE

Above. A fireplace with character fits in perfectly with the pale wood of the parquet floor, the furniture and the trompe-l'oeil woodwork by Nathalie Mahiu. French actor Pierre Arditi crowned this warm decor with sofas designed by Yves Halard and pale curtains that give an added brightness to the living room. The pine desk dates from the 17th century. The antique kilims are flea market finds, and the armchairs are Anne Gayet creations.

Above. Warm hues and candles create an intimate ambience in the home of Yves and Michèle Halard. The decoration of this living room is all about things natural and authentic. It features broad planked, rough pine parquet, the branch of a tree. and a basket overflowing with balls of moss.

The armchairs are covered with a fabric that goes well with the quilt of toile de Jouy hanging on the wall. The low table was designed by Yves Halard.

AROUND THE FIREPLACE

Rustic comfort and a spirit
of Scandinavia prevail at
Michèle Rédélé's home in
Megève, in the French Alps.
The 18th-century timberwork
has been dismantled, plank
by plank, and reassembled
in exactly the same manner.
The coffee table, designed by
Rédélé was made by Alain
Grosset, a Megève blacksmith.
The sofas are covered with a
woolen cloth from Bonneval.
The Manufactor lights add
a contemporary touch.

Above. In Jacques Leguennec's house, a 19th-century English pine fireplace, salvaged and restored, displays a collection of Viennese bronzes and two candlesticks painted in trompe-l'œil from the Atelier J. Leguennec. The wall is covered with a yellow fabric and decorated with a collection of drawings by Garouste, Delacroix and others.

Right. In the home of Corinne Guisez, the fireplace is incorporated in a solid beechwood bookcase. The warmth of the pale wood creates a pleasant, cozy atmosphere.

AROUND THE FIREPLACE

Left. The plaster fireplace of gallery owner Gladys Mougin was created by sculptor Laurence Montano, who came up with a plant motif. The fireplace forms a harmonious whole with the overmantel wall just behind it. The lamp and the bronze box are also by Montano. The early 20th-century Selmer Sheim armchair to the right comes from the Patrick Serraire gallery.

Right. This contemporary fireplace has been painted in stucco by Catherine de Decker. Above it are three "Raku" sculptures by François Belliard, two pictures by Russian painter Victor Kulbak, and a Brazier-Jones candlestick. The chairs are by Cornu & Malcourant.

Above. Kenzo's living room has been decorated with sophisticated sobriety and a touch of the exotic. The gray marble fireplace merges into the pale wall, which is decorated with a Delamarre painting. On the marble surround stand two bronze Japanese tigers. To the left, two Indonesian statues.
Right. This classically inspired apartment—which was entirely redesigned by architect Alain Raynaud—successfully combines

elegance and comfort. The
fireplace is the focal point of the
living room. On either side of it
are terra cotta-style, painted
plaster busts and early 19th-
century prints. By the window,
with its faille curtains, we can
see a Louis XIV armchair
upholstered in silk velvet and
mohair. The wooden lamps come
from Nobilis, and the cushions
are by Simrane. In the
foreground, we see 19th-century
bronzes of Marly horses.

BOOK NOOKS

PARDON THE PUN, BUT BOOKCASES SPEAK VOLUMES ABOUT THE TASTES OF THOSE DISPLAYING BOOKS AND ART ON THEIR SHELVES. THESE PIECES OF FURNITURE NOT ONLY INCREASE AVAILABLE STORAGE SPACE, BUT ALSO SERVE AS FULLY FLEDGED FEATURES OF THE DECOR.

Left. Designer Henri Becq designed these three bookcases, which reach from floor to ceiling. He deliberately set them slightly apart, so as to give space to the shelving. The bookcases are made of rosewood-hued poplar. Around the varnished ash table, three Directoire chairs covered in string linen. The floor lamp is a Modénature creation, and the two small lamps were designed by Julie Prisca. **Above.** In this Left Bank apartment, the oak and mesh bookcases are divided by stucco columns. The armchair, reupholstered in a striped velvet, is a Boussac creation, and the candelabra-type lamp is the work of Annick Clavier.

BOOK NOOKS

The art of living is perfected
in this Greenwich Village
living room. The owner of
this apartment has cleverly
created maximum space from
a minimum of volume.
The rendering that once
covered the walls has been
removed and replaced by
painted wooden planks to make
the room look larger. On the
far wall, picture shelves display
works by Geoffrey Holder and
Le Groumellec. The shelves are
adjacent to a narrow bookcase
that allows the volumes to
remain upright. The television
is set into the wall. On the
coffee table, a collection of
silver candlesticks and an
articulated lamp from Camoin.
The color white is everywhere
and is enhanced by the bright
colors of the pictures.

Above. The harmonious
balance in this Saint-Germain-
des-Prés duplex is the result
of a design by Laurent Bourgois
that was based on a 19th-
century studio work.
The architect-*cum*-interior

designer has emphasized light
and juggled with the mansarded
volumes. The extensive
bookshelves—which fit perfectly
in this living room—were made
by Mac Déco. Behind the
Hugues Chevalier sofa, covered

with a Pierre Frey flannel
fabric, stands a Marina Donati
bronze. Books fill the shelves,
and curios and sculptures are
spread out over the coffee table
by Bertoia. But the room retains
a serene atmosphere because it

has been so perfectly organized. **Above.** This Saint-Germain apartment is quite different. It is made up of things the owners couldn't resist and is furnished exclusively with tactile materials, wood,

marble and whitewash. In its sumptuous volumes, the room manages to display an austere beauty. The bookcases have been painted with the same coating as the walls. Above them, trompe-l'œil

paintings of books, vases and baskets have been added to restore the proportions— which were not always quite right. The "Champagne Cork" chairs come from the Cour Intérieure gallery.

This Neuilly apartment has
been completely redesigned
by Laurent Bourgois.
The bookshelves are made
of painted wood in the
Directoire spirit and are lit
by Dutruc-Rosset wall lights.
The large-stripe sofa stands
on studio parquet made of
broad, dark-varnished planks.

BOOK NOOKS

Left. The New York apartment of the late Bill Blass expresses an extremely personal, and typically neo-Palladian style. The bookshelves, with their stress on sobriety, display both books and art works. Articulated lights in copper-plated brass illuminate the shelves. Various influences—such as ancient China and the Greece of antiquity—are at work here. On the table, among other things, a piece of a Roman mask and a 19th-century bronze.

Right. The central section of this bookcase, which holds hi-fi and video equipment, can revolve on its own axis. Thanks to this movement, one can angle this section and direct it at different parts of the room, or even turn it around so that it is hidden from view. This ingenious invention is by J. Gourvenec.

Above. In Frédéric Méchiche's Marais home, the decor was inspired by the 18th and 19th centuries. The walls of the library are covered with 18th-century woodwork.

In front of the window, the interior designer has put a Napoleon III sofa covered with mauve satin. The old parquet is made of rough oak planks that were found at a

salvage yard. A Moroccan table stands on a small North African rug, the stripes of which echo those of the chairs and chaise lounge. The other chairs are covered with canvas sheet.

Above. In Jacques Leguennec's living room in Paris, near Saint-Germain-des-Prés, the books are arranged by theme in a set of limed oak bookcases that he designed, and that cover almost all of the walls. The two sofas facing each other are covered with canvas sheet. In the middle, two coffee tables bring out the symmetrical effects. In front of the window, a limed oak lectern, also designed by Jacques. The turned wooden lamp has been painted by Alain Ozanne.

Above. Don't be fooled by the simplicity of this living room. The owners were keen to recreate a holiday ambience with light and luminous colors, and thus chose white paint to cover the walls, slatted wooden blinds, and poplar wood, so as to capture as much light as possible. The two bookcases, with their harmonious proportions, create a lovely sense of symmetry. The three sofas are covered in white cloth and imitation leather. They produce an enclosed space together with the piece of furniture in the foreground.

Above. In this apartment beneath the roofs of Paris, architect Laurent Bourgois juggles with contrasting effects created by shades of dark and light. With its double exposure, the living room is beautifully lit and arranged around a symmetrical axis created by the fireplace and the coffee table. Symmetry is also created by the bookcases, the low, armless chairs and the Christian Liaigre sofas. The cushions and flowers add a colorful note to this white ensemble, and they help to highlight pictures and other precious objects.

BOOK NOOKS

This study-*cum*-library also
combines an exercise corner
on the top floor of a 17th-
century Parisian building.
The impressive volume of
this well lit triplex makes it
easy to display a collection
of contemporary works.
as well as one or two older
ones. The bookshelves running
along the glass wall present
this collection. The chairs
are by René Herbst.
On the Jean-Michel Wilmotte
rug stands a desk by Franco
Albini with a Tizio lamp.

87

Left. This warm and inviting hall is a prominent feature of Michel Klein's house. In the oakwood Louis XVI bookcases, the fashion designer has thrown together a disparate range of objects from all over— including photos of American Indians by Curtis and Vietnamese gongs hanging from the pull-out flaps.

Right. This study is devoted to art books and religious canvases from the 17th and 18th centuries. The walls are covered with them. The table is encircled by a set of Hoffmann chairs. In the foreground, a large trestle table makes room for an array of reference books owned by this enthusiastic collector of art.

BOOK NOOKS

In the home of architect and
interior decorator John
Stefanidis, each room
is an extension of the garden.
In the low and narrow central
wing of his English farm,
the hall acts as his library.
It is a thoroughly discreet
library that blends with
its setting and is pleasantly
disguised by hanging geraniums
and daturas. The "Malcontenta"
chairs were designed and
produced by Stefanidis.

Above. Antiques dealer Alexandre Biaggi loves combining objects in ways that are very atypical. In his home, he cultivates a mix of styles that are dear to him. The library, which forms an alcove around the 19th-century desk, features works of art that look right at home alongside books. To the right, a splendid 1930s armchair. **Right.** In the home of this collector of 19th- and 20th-century art, the walls are decorated with pictures and books. The bookshelves have been painted white so that they fade into the background, thus giving the pictures the leading role. Beneath the shelves is a series of Berenice Abbott photos.

Above. Interior decorator Fabienne Villacreces likes unexpected combinations. This 19th-century bookcase offers ample opportunity for artistic daring. For instance, a Limoges china tea set by Arman is placed next to a work by Jean Tinguely.

In the foreground, a 1950s chair found in London, and on the table a colorful cow by Niki de Saint-Phalle. The end result is an eclectic dialogue between the ancient, the modern and the very contemporary. **Right.** For this apartment,

Frédéric Méchiche recreated a past that dates from the late 19th century to Directoire. He added friezes, cornices and moldings to give the living room a personal touch. The mirrors, next to the bookcases bring an extra dimension into play.

ONE BOOKCASE...

Two chrome-plated wall lights by Yves Halard have been fixed to the top of this natural oakwood bookcase. On the shelves are an egg on a stand, turned wooden candlesticks, a stone miniature door, and a hand, horse and mannequin, in wood.

FOUR VARIATIONS

Here, the same bookcase
with the lower doors clad
in chicken wire. The chrome-
plated wall lights by Yves

Halard are fitted to the
sides. The vase with lid
and candle holders are
by Christophe Delcourt.

The inside of the bookcase has now been painted emerald green, while the exterior has been coated with diluted white paint so as to let the grain of the wood show through.

The lower doors feature vertical grooves made with a circular saw. Among the objects arranged on the shelves, we see Vallauris dishes, vases, dice and amphoras.

Within the outer frame of each door of the bookcase, a cross has been scored with very shallow lines, using a circular saw. Two brass wall lights are fixed to the sides. The stelae, moldings and vase come from the Louvre Museum Boutique in Paris. The small pitcher and the ceramic teapot come from the Metropolitan Museum of Art in New York.

WHITE
LIVING ROOMS

WHITE LIVING ROOMS NEVER GO OUT OF FASHION. THEY ARE A CLASSIC; ALL ABOUT LIGHT. IN THEM, LINEN AND CANVAS, STONE AND PALE WOOD COME TOGETHER HARMONIOUSLY. NOW AND THEN, A FEW DASHES OF COLOR ENHANCE THE WHITENESS OF THESE LUMINOUS SPACES.

Left. The owner of this house in the Bahamas designed the living room tables and sofas, which were then made by island craftsmen. Cushions and bolsters covered with white fabric rest on wooden frames. On the wall, models of half hulls found bargain hunting in London, and a carved whale bought in Nantucket. The wooden lamps with their painted brass shades are inspired by amphoras. **Above.** In the home of Monic Fisher, creator of Blanc d'Ivoire, we find a thoroughly laid-back living room. The linen-covered sofa and armchairs come from Desio. The table on the left is covered with a quilted fabric. On it reside finials, a Raphaël Scorbiac sculpture entitled "Le Mouvement," and a lamp. Hanging on the far wall are three photos by Edouard Boubat.

WHITE LIVING ROOMS

Ricardo Bofill defines this cube-shaped room of grandiose dimensions (46 x 46 ft., and 26 ft. from floor to ceiling) that he designed in an old cement works as "domestic, monumental, brutalist and conceptual." The walls and ceilings are made of rough cement. The sofas and seats are covered with white cotton and, the plant boxes are made of painted wood and stainless steel. To the right of the supporting pillar, we can glimpse a white marble sculpture by Bofill.

Above. This duplex, with its double exposure, ivory walls and bleached parquet floors, is an open invitation to light. It was decorated by Monic Fisher. The immaculate sofa is upholstered with linen. The desk, made of granite and wrought iron, contrasts nicely with the furniture, which was all designed by Frédéric Méchiche. The stout, pale oak coffee table

has been hollowed out to conceal a spot. On the wall, a photo of Dora Maar.

Above. This house in Paris gives off a country ambience. It features coir matting on the floor and gray lacquered beams. The sofas are covered with canvas sheet. A Louis XVI commode and a roll-top desk are visible in the back. The painting is from Galerie La Scala.

WHITE LIVING ROOMS

Left. The host of precious objects on display in this collector's living room includes alabaster busts and small clocks on the tables. The walls are covered with blue paneling: the floor with hexagonal tiles. The table is skillfully disguised beneath quilted fabric. The armchairs, belonging to the Louis XV family, have white slipcovers over them. On the walls, a collection of pastels by the painter Helleu.

Right. Variable geometry and a functional spirit dominate interior decorator Carole Fakiel's loft. All the furniture is on casters, and the metal staircase is fitted with large wheels so that it can be pivoted, thus changing the setup of the room. The coffee table design is based on an industrial kit system. The floor is made of parquet from railway cars. It has been given a gray patina and then vitrified. The armchairs come from flea markets and the 1950s stools are Finnish.

WHITE
LIVING ROOMS

In Corsica, the modernism
of a rigorously designed
living room is simple, but
very carefully thought out.
This room—which opens
generously onto the outdoors
through large picture
windows—adopts a spare style.
The living room has beautiful
volumes, but little furniture.
The architect Boguslaw
Brzeczkowski, of the
Groupement d'Etudes
Architecturales (GEA), built
the house entirely in red cedar
to lend it unity. The parquet
has been covered with a high
gloss, gray paint, and the walls
are finished in another very
subtle shade of gray.
The ceilings are white.
The banquette and the
bookcases were designed by
the architect and the owners
as the house was being built.

109

Above. Sumptuous classicism is evident in this brainchild of architects Stephen Sills and James Huniford, near New York. The floor is made of paving stones, conjuring up old streets.

In their effort to maintain symmetry, a bull's eye window was added to the left of the fireplace. The seats are from the Gustavian period. The Regency sofa is upholstered in linen.

Above. In this large living room illuminated by windows opening onto the East River. Empire furniture rubs shoulders with torsos and heads from antiquity. and a Picasso drawing of Marie-Thérèse Walter from the 1930s. The owner, the late Bill Blass, designed the white, silk-covered sofa. The walls are adorned with enamel paint and the parquet is made of mahogany.

WHITE LIVING ROOMS

The English armchairs in this light-filled New York living room are covered with wool cloth. The screen at the far wall is made of narrow strips with gold studded velvet on a limed oak frame. The furniture is of the neoclassical variety, and the white linen curtains are trimmed with a narrow Hellenic frieze. On the floor, an ecru matting has been laid over a dark mahogany parquet.

Above. Suzanne Delarue has a real fondness for white, and likes nothing better than to enhance it with the odd accent of gold and cream. The loggia here is finished off with light curtains, and on the long surface that acts as her desk, the artist has arrayed family photos and two rough sheet metal lights designed by Yves Halard. **Right.** Here, we have a view from below the loggia. On either side of the gilded, wooden Regency mirror are masks by Delarue. Note the single earring. The padded stool has been re-covered with upholstery fabric, and the parquet is painted white.

Inès de la Fressange's apartment
draws its inspiration from the
Gustavian style. The accent is
on softness, with a range of pale
colors, in addition to striped
and squared fabrics. The walls
of this small living room have
been paneled using the wood
from an old straightened
parquet, which was planed and
then polished. The moldings are
made of staff and wood. The
curtains are of striped silk
taffeta. The sofa and low
fireside chair come from
London, as do the cushion
fabrics. On the mantelpiece,
two Gustavian candlesticks in
marble and gilded bronze.
And, in the foreground, two
Pont-Aux-Choux white faience
candlesticks from the shop in
the Museum of Decorative Arts.

117

WHITE
LIVING ROOMS

Catherine Memmi has opted
for three main colors for her
Haussmann-like apartment in
Saint-Germain-des-Prés: matte
white, sandy and black. The
colors go well together and lend
this brightly lit living room a
simple and assertive elegance.
The long sofa is covered in
white cotton cloth. The floor
is covered with a large, black
sisal carpet. The wenge table is
a Catherine Memmi creation.
On it, we see a square ceramic
dish with Moka candles and
photo albums in black nubuck.
On the wall, a painting by
Hilton McConnico.

WHITE
LIVING ROOMS

Right. Yves Taralon's house
is in tune with the seasons.
In winter, the house wraps itself
snugly in double curtains and
creates a warm atmosphere
around solid colors. The sofa is
covered with velvet, while the
wing chairs are upholstered in a
Fardis fabric. The kilim comes
from the Triff Gallery, and the
X-shaped stools are by
Stéphane Deschamps.

Left. When fine weather
returns, white fabrics take
over the room and the kilim is
replaced by coir on the polished
terra cotta floor. The armchairs
and sofas are covered in
Panama fabric. The rug is
made of rattan, and the fire
dogs are by Olivier Gagnère
for the Maeght Gallery.

Useful Addresses

FURNITURE AND ACCESSORIES

ABC CARPET & HOME
(ACCESSORIES, CUSTOM DRAPERY, FURNITURE)
www.abchome.com
P: 212-473-3000

B & B ITALIA
(CONTEMPORARY SOFAS, ARMCHAIRS, TABLES)
www.bebitalia.it
P: 800-872-1697

BAKER FURNITURE
(TRADITIONAL FURNITURE)
www.bakerfurnitue.com
P: 800-59-BAKER

BRITISH KHAKI
(HANDCRAFTED FURNITURE)
www.britishkhaki.com
P: 212-343-2299

CASSINA
(CONTEMPORARY DESIGN FURNITURE)
www.cassinausa.com
P: 800-770-3568

CENTURY
(TRADITIONAL FURNITURE, UPHOLSTERY COLLECTIONS)
www.centuryfurniture.com
P: 800-852-5552

THE CONRAN SHOP
(ACCESSORIES, DESIGN FURNITURE, LIGHTING)
www.conran.com
P: 866-755-9079

CRATE & BARREL
(FURNITURE, LIGHTING, TEXTILES, WINDOW TREATMENTS)
www.crateandbarrel.com
P: 800-967-6696

DENNIS MILLER ASSOCIATES
(DESIGN CHAIRS, TABLES)
www.dennismiller.com
P: 212-684-0070

DONGHIA
(DESIGN FURNITURE, TEXTILES, UPHOLSTERY, WICKER AND RATTAN, TABLES)
www.donghia.com
P: 800-366-4442

ETHAN ALLEN
(HOME FURNISHINGS)
www.ethanallen.com
P: 888-EA-HELP1

GRANGE
(ARMCHAIRS, CABINETRY, SOFAS, WOOD FURNITURE)
www.grange.fr
P: 800-GRANGE-1

GUMPS
(ACCESSORIES, FURNITURE)
www.gumps.com
P: 800-436-4311

HERMAN MILLER
(HOME OFFICE FURNISHINGS)
www.hermanmiller.com
P: 888-443-4357

HICKORY CHAIR
(CLASSIC FURNITURE)
www.hickorychair.com
P: 828-324-1801

IKEA
(ACCESSORIES, FURNITURE, LIGHTING, RUGS)
www.ikea-usa.com

KNOLL
(DESIGN CHAIRS, TABLES, LOUNGE)
www.knoll.com
P: 800-343-5665

LAFCO
(CONTEMPORARY FURNITURE,
ACCESSORIES)
www.lafcony.com
P: 800-362-3677

LES MIGRATEURS
(FURNITURE,
UPHOLSTERY)
www.lesmigrateurs.com
P: 207-846-1430

LINDA HORN
(ANTIQUES)
www.lindahorn.com
P: 800-772-8008

MOLTENI
(CONTEMPORARY
FURNITURE)
www.molteni.it
P: 201-585-9420

OLY
(HANDCRAFTED
FURNITURE, UPHOLSTERY,
ACCESSORIES)
www.olystudio.com
P: 510-644-1870

PIER 1 IMPORTS
(ACCESSORIES,
FURNITURE, WINDOW
TREATMENTS)
www.pier1.com
P: 800-245-4595

PIERCE MARTIN
(WICKER, RATTAN AND
IRON FURNISHINGS,
ACCESSORIES)
www.piercemartin.com
P: 800-334-8701

POTTERY BRAN
(ACCESSORIES, FURNITURE,
LAMPS, WINDOW
COVERINGS)
www.potterybarn.com
P: 888-779-5176

POLIFORM USA
(CONTEMPORARY
FURNITURE)
www.poliformusa.com
P: 888-POLIFORM

PUCCI
(CONTEMPORARY
FURNITURE)
www.ralphpucci.com
P: 212-633-0452

REPERTOIRE
(CONTEMPORARY FURNITURE)
www.repertoire.com
P: 212-219-8159

RESTORATION HARDWARE
(ACCESSORIES, FURNITURE,
WINDOW TREATMENTS)
www.restorationhardware.com
P: 800-762-1005

ROCHE BOBOIS
(PERIOD AND STYLE
FURNITURE)
www.roche-bobois.com
P: 800-972-8375

STOREHOUSE
(FURNITURE,
UPHOLSTERY)
www.storehouse.com
P: 888-STOREHOUSE

FABRICS

BERGAMO
(LUXURY FABRICS)
www.bergamofabrics.com
P: 914-665-0800

BOUSSAC
(LUXURY FABRICS)
www.boussac-tadini.fr
P: 866-268-7722

BRUNSCHWIG & FILS
(FABRICS, HOME
FURNISHINGS,
LAMPS)
www.brunschwig.com

F. SCHUMACHER & CO.
(FABRICS, HOME
FASHIONS, WALLPAPER)
www.fschumacher.com
P: 800-332-3384

J. ROBERT SCOTT
(TEXTILES, ACCESSORIES)
www.jrobertscott.com
P: 800-322-4910

KRAVET
(FABRICS, TRIMMINGS)
www.kravet.com
P: 800-648-KRAV

PIERRE FREY
(LUXURY FABRICS)
www.pierrefrey.com
P: 212-213-3099

WAVERLY
(FABRICS, WALLPAPER)
www.waverly.com
P: 800-423-5881

CARPETS & RUGS

ABC CARPET & HOME
(LUXURY CARPETS, FABRICS)
www.abchome.com
P: 212-473-3000

CAPEL
(AREA RUGS)
www.capelrugs.com
P: 800-382-6574

CALVIN KLEIN
(AREA RUGS)
P: 800-294-7978

COURISTAN
(HANDMADE AND
BROADLOOM RUGS)
www.couristan.com
P: 800-223-6186

ENDLESS KNOT
(CLASSIC,
CONTEMPORARY,
TIBETAN RUGS)
www.endlessknotrugs.com
P: 800-910-3000

HABIDECOR
(LUXURY RUGS)
www.habidecorusa.com
P: 800-588-8565

KARASTAN
(LUXURY CARPETS
AND RUGS)
www.karastan.com
P: 800-234-1120

**M & M DESIGN
INTERNATIONAL**
(ORIENTAL AND
CUSTOM RUGS)
www.mandmgallery.com
P: 516-456-0681

**MICHAEL AZIZ
ORIENTAL RUGS**
(PAKISTAN RUGS)
www.michaelazizrugs.com
P: 212-686-8755

NOURISON
(HANDMADE RUGS)
www.nourison.com
P: 800-223-1110

ODEGARD
(LUXURY CARPETS)
www.odegardinc.com
P: 800-670-8836

TILES

AMTICO
(CERAMIC, GLASS,
GRANITE, MARBLE,
MOSAICS, SHELL,
STONE)
www.amtico.com
P: 800-268-4260

ANN SACKS
(CERAMIC, GLASS, MOSAICS,
STONE, PORCELAIN)
www.annsacks.com
P: 800-278-8453

ARTISTIC TILE
(CERAMIC, GLASS, MOSAICS,
STONE, PORCELAIN)
www.artistictile.com
P: 800-260-8646

BISAZZA
(GLASS, MOSAICS)
www.bisazzausa.com

COUNTRY FLOORS
(MOSAICS, TERRA COTTA)
www.countryfloors.com
P: 800-311-9995

DUPONT
(TILING)
www.corian.com
P: 800-4-CORIAN

EMAUX DE BRIARE
(TILING)
www.emauxdebriare.com
P: 516-931-5924

HASTINGS TILE
(GLASS, MOSAICS,
PORCELAIN, STONE)
www.hastingstilebath.com
P: 516-379-3500

PARIS CERAMICS
DECORATIVE CERAMIC,
ANTIQUE TERRA COTTA,
MOSAICS)
www.parisceramics.com
P: 888-845-3487

WALKER ZANGER
(CERAMIC, GLASS, METAL,
STONE, TERRA COTTA)
www.walkerzanger.com
P: 877-611-0199

LIGHTING SPECIALISTS

ROBERT ABBEY
(LIGHTING DESIGN)
www.robertabbey.com
P: 828-322-3480

ARTEMIDE
(LIGHTING DESIGN)
www.artemide.com
P: 631-694-9292

CX DESIGN
(LIGHTING DESIGN)
P: 888-431-4242

FLOS
(LIGHTING DESIGN)
www.flos.net
P: 800-939-3567

NAMBE
(LIGHTING DESIGN,
ACCESSORIES)
www.nambe.com
P: 800-443-0339

JAMIE YOUNG
(LIGHTING DESIGN,
ACCESSORIES)
www.jamieyoung.com
P: 888-671-5883

WE WOULD LIKE TO THANK THE OWNERS, DECORATORS AND INSTITUTIONS THAT HAVE WELCOMED *ELLE DECOR* COLLABORATORS FOR THEIR REPORTAGES:

PIERRE ARDITI, MAÏME ARNODIN, MEHMET BAY, HENRI BECQ, NINA AND PHILIPPE BENOIT, ALEXANDRE BIAGGI, BILL BLASS, MARC BLONDEAU, RICARDO BOFILL, CAROLINE BONTE, LAURENT BOURGOIS, BOGUSLAW BRZECZKOWSKI (G.E.A.), CHRISTINA AND ROLAND BURRUS, MANUEL CANOVAS, DAVID CHAMPION, ANTHONY COLLETT, AGNES COMAR, MR. DECELLE, MARIE-ELISABETH DELACARTE, SUZANNE DELARUE, MRS. EHRINGER, CAROLE FAKIEL, MONIC FISHER, LUC FOURNOL, YVELINE AND PATRICK FRECHE, INES DE LA FRESSANGE, JEAN GALVANI, ZEYNEP GARAN, YVES GASTOU, J. GOURVENEC, CORINNE GUISEZ, MICHELE AND YVES HALARD, WILLIAM HALDRON, ANOUSKA HEMPEL, JAMES HUNIFORD, LIONEL JADOT, JOSEPH, KENZO, DANIEL KIENER, MICHEL KLEIN, PATRICIA AND ERIC LAIGNEAU, ANNA AND GUNTHER LAMBERT, HUBERT LE GALL, JACQUES LEGUENNEC, CHARLES MATTON, FREDERIC MECHICHE, MADO AND JEAN-LOUIS MELLERIO, CATHERINE MEMMI, JOELLE MORTIER VALLAT, GLADYS MOUGIN, REGIS PAGNEZ, JULIE PRISCA, ALAIN RAYNAUD, MICHELE REDELE, JANE ROBERTS, JACQUES-EMILE RUHLMANN, BRIGITTE SEMTOB, STEPHEN SILLS, PHILIPPE STARCK, JOHN STEFANIDIS, YVES TARALON, REMI TESSIER, AUDE DE THUIN, AXEL VERHOUSTRAETEN, AXEL VERVOORDT, FABIENNE VILLACRECES.

Photographs:

Guillaume de Laubier: pp. 8, 9, 12-13, 14, 26, 28-35 (top), 36-37, 41, 44, 45, 50, 52-60, 62, 66-70, 77, 81, 83, 88, 89, 93, 105, 106, 110, 120
Marianne Haas: pp. 10, 11, 22, 23, 27, 40, 49, 61, 63, 64-65, 71, 72, 76, 80, 90-91, 92, 94, 101, 111, 114, 115, 118-119
Jacques Dirand: pp. 16-17, 42-43, 46, 48, 82, 84, 86-87, 102-103, 104, 108-109, 116-117
Séline Keller: pp. 18, 19, 21, 24-25, 85
Alain Gelberger: pp. 96, 97, 98, 99
Patrice Pascal: pp. 38-39, 78-79
Edouard Sicot: pp. 74-75, 100
Philippe Costes: pp. 16-17, 121
Gilles de Chabaneix: pp. 15, 51, 95
William Haldron: pp. 112-113
Daniel Kessler: p. 35 (bottom)
Gilles Trillard: p. 73

Words and style:

Marie-Claire Blanckaert: pp. 8, 9, 11, 12-13, 14, 16-17, 18, 19, 21, 23, 24-25, 27, 32-37, 40, 41, 42-43, 44, 47, 49, 50, 52-70, 72, 73, 74-75, 77, 81, 82, 83, 88, 89, 93, 101, 104, 105, 106, 118-119, 120
Barbara Bourgois: pp. 20, 38-39, 63, 71, 78-79, 85, 96, 97, 98, 99
Françoise Labro: pp. 26, 28-29, 30, 31, 84, 86-87, 108-109
François Baudot: pp. 80, 90-91, 102-103, 110, 111, 112-113, 116-117
Catherine Scotto: pp. 16-17, 22, 121
Laure Verchère: pp. 10, 92, 94
Jacqueline Demornex: pp. 114, 115
Marie-Claude Dumoulin: pp. 20, 51
Marie Kalt: p. 95
Gérard Pussey: p. 76.
Geneviève Dortignac: p. 48

Elle Decor (U.S.) and *Elle Décoration* (France) are both imprints of the Hachette Filipacchi group.
The content of this book was taken solely from *Elle Décoration* and appeared only in France.

**Under the direction of
Jean Demachy**

Editorial
Marie-Claire Blanckaert

Art Direction
Anne-Marie Chéret

Editing
Nicolas Rabeau

Photo Research
Geneviève Tartrat

Text Research
Sandrine Hess